THE CHRISTMAS CAROL MIRACLE

Illustrations by Nancy Deyhle

ABINGDON PRESS
Nashville & New York

THE CHRISTMAS CAROL MIRACLE

Luise Putcamp jr.

THE
CHRISTMAS
CAROL
MIRACLE

The town where it happened was not the kind of town you'd choose for a miracle. It was sur-rounded by dust and wind in West Texas. All you could see for miles around was mesquite and oil wells and the town's one skyscraper, the Derrick Building. Both the town and the building were more

or less named for Gus Derek, who owned all those oil wells.

December in Derrick, Texas was not like December on the Christmas cards. The cold there was the kind that makes people go around cross and runny-nosed and mumbling about antifreeze. It's no wonder the people of Derrick, if they thought of miracles at all, thought of them in connection with somewhere else altogether—a little picturesque village in the Swiss Alps maybe, but certainly not Derrick, Texas.

But Derrick, Texas had Christmas, and its Santa Claus was Gus Derek, a lean, weatherworn man who didn't look the part but played it every Christmas by giving a substantial batch of oil royalties to the school whose choir sang best at the yearly carol festival. There were people who said Gus Derek gave the money not because he liked Christmas carols, but because he wanted to take it off his income tax in April. This year he had outdone himself—the prize was $10,000.

Derrick had four schools. There was the high school. There was the grand new grammar school on Gusher Hill where the reek of oil was richer than anyplace else in town. There was the old grammar school, a sturdy building in a sturdy part of town called Driller's Dell. And there was the orphanage. Not once had the orphanage choir won the Christmas money from Gus Derek. And this was a sad

thing, because the orphanage was the one school in town that didn't have a taxpayer to its name.

The prosperous people of Derrick, Texas didn't much like to think about the orphanage. For one thing it reminded them of the lean days in Derrick, between oil booms. That's when the orphanage started, and there was something of a mystery about who started it and where it got the money to go on. Some said an old scoundrel who got rich on shoddy, man-killing oil-field machinery later got religion and decided to do some good for a change. There were a lot of old scoundrels around Derrick, but folks said that this one lived out of town, and every year a check arrived at the orphanage in a registered enve-lope from an out-of-town law firm.

The check must have been getting smaller and smaller, because lately the orphanage looked more and more like a poor relation tagging at the heels of a rich oilman.

And the year the miracle happened the men

who ran Derrick were thinking very un-Christmas-like thoughts about the orphanage. They were plot-ting to get rid of the old firetrap once and for all. As a matter of fact, it stood right where the city wanted to put a big new park, with a swimming pool and maybe even an outdoor theater for a little culture. And the men who ran Derrick told them-selves that after all, the orphans would really be better off in a state institution. They'd really be doing the orphans a favor in the long run by getting them out of Derrick, Texas. And so the men put their heads together.

Over at the orphanage everybody was too busy getting ready for the carol festival to worry about the old building. By now the children all knew just where the roof leaked and where the blue northers whistled between the warped boards. It was a kind of game avoiding the drips and drafts. But the best game of all was the carol festival. The children at the orphanage thought about it all year, the way other children think of Santa Claus. With the first frost each fall they began thumbing through the tattered songbook to decide what they would sing that year. They always ended up choosing the same song— "O Come, All Ye Faithful." And if they made "O come, let us adore Him" sound kind of like a football yell, it was because they thought the

little Christ child would like it that way. They always thought of Him as one of them. It's true He wasn't an orphan, but wasn't it also true that He too had no home?

Mrs. Motherwell, the ample, gray-haired woman who ran the orphanage, would start the children singing with her little pitch pipe. And her assistant, thin, bright-eyed Miss Princh, would beat time on a table with a ruler.

This particular Christmas, right when carol practicing was at its height—and money was at its lowest—the orphanage got a new orphan. His name was Christopher, and nobody knew how old he was for sure. They'd look at his spindly arms and legs and his tousled head and think he must be almost seven. And then they'd look into his white face and his big dark eyes and think Christopher must be at least a hundred years old.

Nobody knew exactly where he'd come from, either. It wasn't the kind of orphanage that asks questions and fills out forms. Some grimy men from the oil field brought Christopher in one day. They said his mother had died years ago, when he

was born, and Chris had been bumming around the oil country with his daddy—until just last week. Last week his daddy had been killed in a drilling-rig accident.

So Mrs. Motherwell took a blanket from her own bed, and Miss Princh went without her stew that night, and Christopher stayed.

But at night Christopher huddled under his blanket as if nothing in the world would ever keep him warm again. And in the daytime he hung back, silently watching the other children play their noisy, makeshift games. The only thing in the orphanage that made Christopher smile was Christmas-carol practice.

He would hover nearby like a little starved bird and listen as the pitch pipe sounded and the thin, sweet voices of the other children turned the drab room into a room of sudden riches. And Mrs. Motherwell, listening, thought this was the best choir the orphanage ever had. Surely this was the choir that would win the prize at the carol festival.

But one day Christopher opened his pale little mouth to join in on "O come, let us adore Him." Mrs. Motherwell smiled in delight that soon turned to dismay. Because Christopher had a voice like the chirping of a frog. What was worse, he couldn't carry a tune—not at all. As he sang, the rest of the children began turning to each other and making faces. Somebody giggled. Mrs. Motherwell shook her head, and somehow the carol was finished.

When Christopher saw that carol practice was over for the day, he scuffled out the door. Mrs. Motherwell turned to the other children.

"We must never laugh at Christopher," she told them. "We must pretend his singing is the sweetest

of all, because singing Christmas carols is the only thing that makes Christopher smile."

And the children nodded their heads solemnly. They knew that a smile in an orphanage is a precious thing.

So day after day Christopher sang with them, his hoarse voice sounding over all the rest. And not one of the children even blinked an eye or quirked the corner of a mouth.

Things were going well until the letter came. It was written in rusty, legal-sounding words and signed in the name of the city commission. What it said was simply this: The city of Derrick, Texas was condemning the orphanage building as unsafe— a menace to the welfare of Derrick. After the first of the year, the building would have to be torn down.

Mrs. Motherwell looked at Miss Princh. What could they do? The answer was "Nothing." Because Mrs. Motherwell and Miss Princh knew something that nobody else in Derrick knew—something that would have made the men who ran Derrick click their high boot heels for joy. This year the registered envelope from the out-of-town law firm had not held a check. It had held a letter saying there would be no more checks—the old scoundrel (the letter called him his right name) had died and there was no more money. He'd given it all to the orphanage over the years.

Mrs. Motherwell and Miss Princh had told each other that if they could hang on a while longer without the checks, maybe they could find another old scoundrel with an uneasy conscience. Or maybe they—but they needed time.

"Would $10,000 build a new orphanage?" asked Mrs. Motherwell, almost to herself. "Because if we could stay here just a little longer—"

"No, it wouldn't," said Miss Princh, who had been thinking the same thing. "But it might fix the leaks in the roof and plug up the cracks between the warped boards. And surely that would satisfy the city for a while."

"It's the best choir the orphanage ever had," said Mrs. Motherwell.

"Except for Christopher," said Miss Princh.

Their thoughts hung like the frost of their breathing in the cold room.

"You'll just have to find some way to tell him he can't sing with the rest," said Miss Princh.

"Perhaps if I explained to him—" said Mrs. Motherwell.

She called Christopher in. All she could see was the top of his head, because as usual Christopher was looking at his toes.

"Christopher," she said gently, "I have something important to tell you. It's about the Christmas carols."

He looked up at her then with his big dark eyes. And the light on his face made her forget the rattle of his harsh little voice. She couldn't think of the words to say, so instead she said, "We must all try to sing our best this year." And Christopher nodded his head very hard.

Afterward she decided to tell the other children. She told them about the letter from the city of Derrick that said the orphanage building must be torn down. She told them they were the best choir the orphanage had ever had—the one that might win the $10,000 from Gus Derek. Then she told them that she couldn't tell Christopher not to sing with the rest.

All the children looked at Mrs. Motherwell in silence. Then one of the smallest said, "But Christopher always spoils the song."

The other children turned to scowl at her, and she meekly put her hand over her mouth.

And though not one of the children said another word, Mrs. Motherwell could see plainly on their faces that they didn't want her to tell Christopher, that they couldn't sing without him. And for the first time since the letter came, for one big moment, Mrs. Motherwell didn't feel sad or worried.

The high school auditorium was decorated with pine branches and red and green ribbon for the carol festival. Most of the people crowded in on Christmas Eve because their children—or their grandchildren, or nieces, or nephews—were singing in the choirs. (No one, of course, came especially to hear the orphans.)

But a lot of people came to the carol festival for rather odd reasons.

For instance, there was old Mrs. Bittrell. To her Christmas meant only toes stepped on in depart-

ment stores and a postman who came later each day. But she *did* like to be around people. And people *did* come to the carol festival.

Then there was the town's banker, Mr. Skrind, who came only because his wife made him come— it was simply the right thing to do, my dear.

And there were people who came just to get in

out of the cold, or so they wouldn't have to sit at home one more night looking at each other.

And of course Gus Derek came, in his hand-tooled boots and his solid-gold-derrick cuff links because, after all, he was giving the prize.

The garble of voices in the auditorium hushed abruptly as the lights went dim and the curtain went up.

The high school choir sang first, and everybody whispered that here was a fine-looking bunch of young people. Their leader, plump Mrs. Credenza, put on an even better show than usual as she waved them through "God Rest Ye Merry, Gentlemen." Everybody knew the high school wanted the $10,000, so it could buy new uniforms and equip-ment for the football team.

Next came the rosy-cheeked children from the Driller's Dell grammar school. They'd been work-ing all year on a secret, and it turned out to be some painstaking four-part harmony on "O Little Town of Bethlehem." It wasn't so much the harmony anyway as the idea of the thing, everybody agreed. Bless their little hearts for trying so hard! Certainly

the children of Driller's Dell deserved the $10,000 to build a new school library.

And everyone gasped with pleasure as the Gusher Hill grammar school choir made its entrance. The children marched down both aisles in snowy robes, carrying candles as they sang an old French Christmas carol—and in the original French, mind you! It wasn't as if they actually needed the $10,000, but they certainly deserved it this year.

When the curtain rose on the orphanage choir, a lot of people were getting up to leave. After all, it was just those orphans, and word had got around that thank goodness, they probably wouldn't be here next year.

Miss Princh stood in the wings, twisting her thin hands together. Out on the stage Mrs. Motherwell sounded the pitch pipe for the children.

They didn't sing with a piano—after all, they never practiced with one. They didn't wear snowy robes, but their hair was brushed, and their cut-down overalls and skimpy dresses were painfully clean and every one of them had shoes on. Even Christopher. At the last minute Mrs. Motherwell had turned up a presentable pair to fit him, and there he stood, in the front row.

Mrs. Motherwell imagined for one twisting in stant how it would be when Christopher started singing. She closed her eyes tight. And then she lifted her hand for the singing to begin.

"O come, all ye faithful!" sang the thin sweet voices of the orphans, all starting at once, all close together like the silver pipes of an organ, sounding even better in the big auditorium than they had in the little room at the orphanage. Mrs. Motherwell and Miss Princh listened in vain for the hoarse voice of Christopher, and as they listened, the miracle happened at Derrick, Texas.

One voice climbed above the others with a sound like bells, like birds never heard before, the sound that starlight would make if light had sound, the voice of love, if love had a voice.

The people who were standing took no step, and the people who were still sitting drew no breath. One by one the other children from the orphanage stopped singing and turned to listen to this voice that sang, "O come, let us adore Him" not like a

football yell, but like an invitation to the most won-
derful birthday party in the world. And as Christopher stood there, singing all alone, some strange
things happened.

Old Mrs. Bittrell suddenly remembered that
Christmas was something besides stepped-on toes and
late postmen. When she was a little girl, there had
been a crib carved of wood and a tiny wax Baby
with a gentle face.

Mr. Skrind, the banker, discovered with con-
siderable surprise that he never wanted the carol
festival to end—it was better than watching football
on television, or sleeping on the couch after Sunday
dinner, even better than foreclosing mortgages.

And Gus Derek, in his hand-tooled boots and
solid-gold-derrick cuff links, thought of the one thing
he had vowed never to think about, the one thing no
one else in Derrick, Texas knew. Long ago *he* had
been a boy from an orphanage, in cut-down overalls
and a pair of shoes bought for somebody else.

The voice stopped, and for a moment there was
a shivering silence. Then people began walking
quickly toward the stage.

The judges, of course, were hustling to tell Mrs. Motherwell that the orphanage choir had won the prize.

Old Mrs. Bittrell wanted to get a better look at that boy who sang. There was something about his face that reminded her of the little wax Baby's face of long ago.

Mr. Skrind headed for the stage because he saw Gus Derek heading there too, and he wanted to ask whether Derek didn't think everyone had been a little hasty about condemning the orphanage building.

And Gus Derek, closing in on the dense little

cluster of people around Christopher, was wondering just how much it would cost to build a new orphanage on a better piece of land—and put in a piano besides.

Christopher looked around with bright eyes. There was pink in his cheeks, and for the first time you could tell how old he was. Seven was about right.

"But Christopher," Mrs. Motherwell and Miss Princh were saying almost at once, "why didn't you sing that way before?"

His face was still puzzled, but it glowed like a candle as he told them.

"I didn't sing!" he said. "I knew my voice wasn't pretty like the other children's voices, and I decided not to spoil the song. I just moved my mouth in time to the words . . . I wasn't really singing at all!"

ILLUSTRATOR AND DESIGNER: Nancy Deyhle

TYPE: Kenntonian
12 pt. leaded 2 pts.

TYPESETTER: Western Typesetting Company

MANUFACTURER: Parthenon Press

PRINTING PROCESS: Offset—1 color

PAPER: Body—80# Mountie Matte
Endsheets—75# Talisman Text Buckskin
printed letterpress—1 color.

BINDING: Phillip G. Whitman—Diago Gold 28-W-92